THE
100+
SERIES™

Reproducible Activities

Daily Warmups

Math Problems & Puzzles

Grade 1

Published by Instructional Fair • TS Denison
an imprint of

Mc Graw Hill **Children's Publishing**

Editors: Alyson Kieda, Linda Triemstra, Bruce Walker

 **Children's Publishing**

Published by Instructional Fair • TS Denison
An imprint of McGraw-Hill Children's Publishing
Copyright © 2003 McGraw-Hill Children's Publishing

Send all inquiries to:
McGraw-Hill Children's Publishing
3195 Wilson Drive NW
Grand Rapids, Michigan 49544

Daily Warmups: Math Problems & Puzzles—grade 1
ISBN: 0-7424-1791-3

1 2 3 4 5 6 7 8 9 PHXBK 08 07 06 05 04 03
The McGraw-Hill Companies

Table of Contents

NCTM Standards	Problem Number
Number and Operations	4, 8, 9, 11, 24, 25, 30, 31, 33, 35, 42, 44, 46, 47, 51, 53, 55, 58, 61, 66, 68, 71, 74, 75, 78, 79, 83, 85, 86, 88, 89, 95, 103, 107, 112, 113, 116, 117, 118, 122, 123, 126, 128, 135, 151, 157, 158, 162, 165, 167, 171, 173, 176, 179, 180, 185, 188, 192, 194, 196, 200, 204, 205, 207, 210, 212, 214, 217, 218, 221, 224, 225, 227, 229
Algebra	16, 20, 26, 37, 59, 76, 81, 91, 93, 106, 110, 114, 119, 124, 138, 145, 156, 169, 189, 198, 211, 230, 232
Geometry	2, 10, 13, 17, 32, 41, 52, 60, 62, 96, 100, 104, 127, 129, 134, 137, 141, 147, 154, 174, 184
Measurement	1, 3, 14, 19, 28, 38, 48, 54, 57, 64, 80, 82, 84, 87, 90, 92, 94, 98, 99, 102, 108, 109, 115, 121, 131, 133, 136, 139, 144, 146, 152, 159, 161, 163, 172, 177, 181, 186, 190, 193, 195, 206, 209, 215, 219, 231, 233
Probability and Statistics	12, 21, 34, 36, 49, 69, 97, 101, 120, 149, 164, 168, 199
Problem Solving	5, 18, 39, 43, 50, 56, 125, 130, 140, 142, 143, 148, 155, 160, 178, 183, 187, 191, 201, 203, 208, 213, 216, 222, 228
Logical Reasoning	6, 22, 23, 29, 40, 72, 105, 132, 182, 197, 220, 223, 234
Patterns and Functions	7, 15, 27, 45, 63, 65, 67, 70, 73, 77, 111, 150, 153, 166, 170, 202, 226

Introduction

This book is one in a series of books from kindergarten through grade 8. Each book provides a wide variety of challenging and engaging grade-appropriate problems and puzzles from all areas of the math curriculum. Each book contains 234 problems and puzzles, one for each day of the school year plus more. All are keyed to the appropriate NCTM standards, and many are designed for hands-on problem solving using common classroom manipulatives. Several problems call for the use of tangrams. For your convenience, we have included a reproducible set on page 5. Other problems call for protractors, dice, pentominoes, and calculators. However, most problems require only paper and pencil and a little brain power.

Each page contains two problems or puzzles. The problems are reproducible and are suitable for overhead use. Most offer ample space for problem solving. The problems and puzzles in this book are designed to be solved within 15 minutes, but most will take 5 minutes or less. These problems are great for use as early-morning warmups or for the beginning of math class and can be worked independently or in groups. You can also assign problems as homework or as a math lab activity. Another idea is to use these problems in contests. Which group or individual will be the first to solve the problem?

Work through a few problems with your students before they begin to work independently or in a group. As you do so, it's important to model a problem-solving process. Stress that many problems have multiple solutions. Then, watch as your students grow and develop their own problem-solving strategies and gain a new appreciation for math.

Tangrams

0-7424-1791-3 *Daily Warmups*

Measurement

Estimate how long each object is: a pencil, a book, and your desk. Then use a ruler to measure each object. How long is each item?

Geometry

Connect the dots to copy the pattern.

Measurement

How many pennies make a dollar?

How many nickels make a dollar?

How many dimes make a dollar?

How many quarters make a dollar?

Number and Operations

Add.

1 + 3 =

1 + 1 =

1 + 2 =

1 + 4 =

Problem Solving

Use the clues to find how old each child is.

 Brandon is 2 years older than Emily.

 Latoya is 3 years older than Brandon.

 Emily is 4 years old.

Logical Reasoning

Mei and her friends are in line at the museum of natural history. Find the order that they are in.

Mei is between Amalie and Matt.

Matt is next to Mei.

Matt is not first in line.

Patterns and Functions

Fill in the missing number.

4   5   6   ____

7   ____   9   10

1   ____   3   4

Number and Operations

Circle the greater number.

6 3   0 6   7 4

Number and Operations

Add.

$2 + 2 =$

$3 + 1 =$

$1 + 3 =$

$0 + 4 =$

Geometry

Match each shape with the correct word.

triangle   rectangle   square   circle

 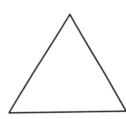 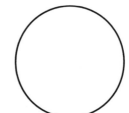 

Number and Operations

Subtract.

$3 - 2 =$

$3 - 3 =$

$2 - 1 =$

$3 - 1 =$

Statistics

Read the graph. Then answer the questions.
Which fruit is the most popular?
Which fruit is the least popular?
How many people said grapes are their favorite fruit?

Favorite Fruits

	Strawberries	Apples	Oranges	Bananas	Grapes
5					
4					
3					
2					
1					

Geometry

Match each shape with the correct word.

diamond

triangle

circle

oval

Measurement

Write the times shown on each clock below.

_____ _____ _____ _____

Patterns and Functions

Fill in the missing numbers.

17 ____   19 ____

11 ____   ____ 14

____ 7   ____ 9

Algebra

In each problem, use three of the four numbers given below to solve each problem. You also must insert the addition and subtraction signs.

Example: 15 + 3 − 12 = 6

Numbers: 12, 5, 3, 15

____ ____ ____ = 0

____ ____ ____ = 8

0-7424-1791-3 *Daily Warmups*

Geometry

Copy each design.

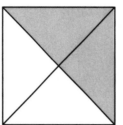 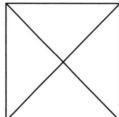 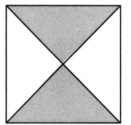 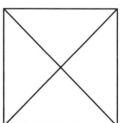

Problem Solving

Color the exact number of coins needed to buy a candy bar that costs $0.35.

10¢	1¢	1¢
5¢	25¢	25¢

0-7424-1791-3 *Daily Warmups*

Measurement

Fill in the calendar for this month.
Mark any special days.

						(Name of Month)
Sunday	Monday	Tuesday	Wednesday	Thursday	Friday	Saturday

Algebra

Find the rule. Then write the missing
numbers in the OUT row.

IN	3	2	7	4	8	5
OUT	5	4	9	6		

0-7424-1791-3 *Daily Warmups*

Statistics

Write the value of each set of tally marks.

_____   _____   _____

Logical Reasoning

Cross out the thing in each row that does not belong.
Explain your answer.

0-7424-1791-3 _Daily Warmups_

Logical Reasoning

Use the clues to find how many children are on the baseball team.

 Clue 1   There is an odd number of children.

 Clue 2   There are more than 6 children.

 Clue 3   There are fewer than 10 children.

 Clue 3   There are not 9 children.

Number and Operations

Write in the numbers in the tens place and the ones place.

4 tens, 6 ones   _____   _____ = _____

5 tens, 7 ones   _____   _____ = _____

3 tens, 8 ones   _____   _____ = _____

Number and Operations

Which number is greater? Draw a square around the greater number.

55   or   62

91   or   19

Which number is smaller? Draw a square around the smaller number.

82   or   56

42   or   43

Algebra

Find the rule. Then fill in the missing numbers in the OUT row.

IN	5	7	8	6	10	14
OUT	10	12	13	11		

0-7424-1791-3 *Daily Warmups*

Patterns and Functions

Fill in the missing numbers.

27 ____   29 ____

23 ____   ____ 26

____   ____ 21 22

Measurement

Measure each shoe using an inch ruler.

____ inches   ____ inches   ____ inches

Logical Reasoning

Cross out the thing in each row that does not belong. Explain your answer.

Number and Operations

Write the numbers that belong in the tens place and the ones place.

57 = ___ tens ___ ones

15 = ___ tens ___ ones

65 = ___ tens ___ ones

0-7424-1791-3 Daily Warmups

Number and Operations

Count each group. Write the total.
Circle the greater number of each set of fruit.

Geometry

Look around your classroom. Find as many
examples as you can of

triangles.

squares.

circles.

rectangles.

Number and Operations

Look at the diagrams below. Then fill in the blanks.

_____ out of _____ are white.

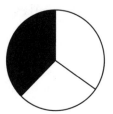

_____ out of _____ is black.

Statistics

Write the value of each group of tally marks.

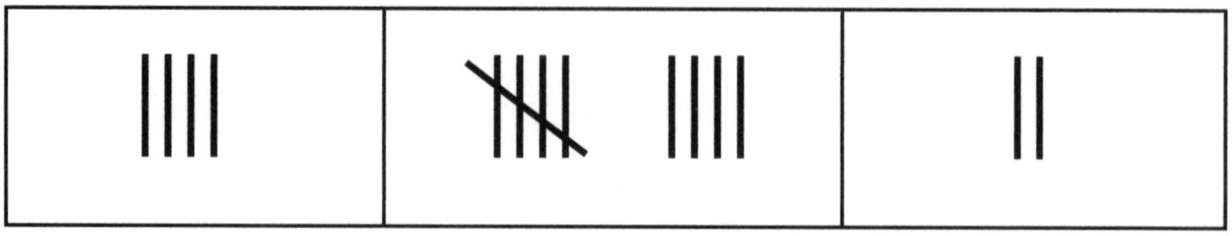

IIII	� IIII	II

_____   _____   _____

0-7424-1791-3 *Daily Warmups*

Number and Operations

There are 4 dogs. Each dog has 3 bones. How many bones do the dogs have altogether?

Statistics

Count how many legs, wings, and tails each set of animals has. Then write the correct number in each column.

Legs	Wings	Tails

Algebra

Find the rule. Then add the missing numbers in the OUT row.

IN	9	7	8	4	10	12
OUT	6	4	5	1		

Measurement

Find and measure each of the items listed. Write the length of each item in centimeters.

your favorite pencil _____

your glue bottle _____

your scissors _____

your calculator _____

0-7424-1791-3 *Daily Warmups*

Problem Solving

Use the clues to find the number.

 The number is between 12 and 15.

 The number is closer to 12 than to 15.

Logical Reasoning

Color each set of triplets the same.

0-7424-1791-3 *Daily Warmups*

Geometry

Look around your classroom and find as many examples as you can of

cubes.

cylinders.

Number and Operations

Count each group. Write the total number in each set of fruit. Then circle the greater number.

0-7424-1791-3 *Daily Warmups*

Problem Solving

Use the clues to solve the puzzle.

 **Clue 1**   Melissa has 10 toy bears.

Clue 2   There are 2 more white bears than brown bears.

How many bears of each color are there?

Number and Operations

Draw a circle around the set that has more.

Draw a circle around the set that has less.

Patterns and Functions

Using tangrams, make the pattern shown below. Now make up your own pattern with the tangrams.

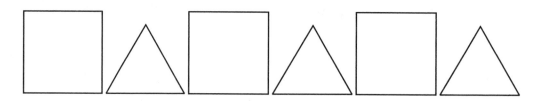

Number and Operations

Draw a circle around the picture that shows thirds.

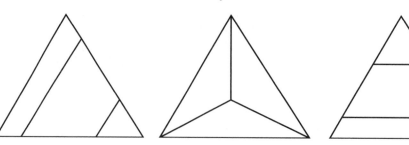

0-7424-1791-3 *Daily Warmups*

Number and Operations

What is the value of the coins shown below?

Measurement

Write the time shown on each clock below.

_____   _____   _____   _____

     0-7424-1791-3 *Daily Warmups*

Statistics

Which question would not be a good survey question?

What is your favorite game?
How many brothers and sisters do you have?
What is your name?
How old are you?

Explain why the question isn't a good survey question.

Problem Solving

Use the clues to find the number.

Clue 1 The number is an odd number.

Clue 2 The number is between 40 and 50.

Clue 3 The number is closer to 40 than it is to 50.

0-7424-1791-3 *Daily Warmups*

Number and Operations

Write the fraction for each figure.

_____ out of _____ is white.

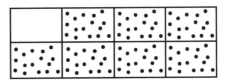

_____ out of _____ are black.

Geometry

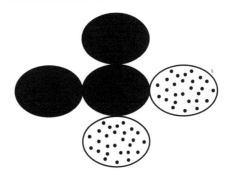

Connect the dots to copy each pattern.

Number and Operations

Add or subtract.

7 + 8 =

11 − 5 =

5 + 9 =

8 − 4 =

Measurement

Write whether the things listed below are closer to the length of a centimeter or a meter.

the width of the classroom door

the width of your pencil

the width of your jump rope

the length of your bicycle

0-7424-1791-3 *Daily Warmups*

Number and Operations

Write the value of the coins shown below.

Problem Solving

Taisha and 4 of her friends each have 2 pears. How many pears do they have in all?

Measurement

Use a centimeter ruler to measure each ice cream cone.

_____ cm   _____ cm   _____ cm

Number and Operations

Add.

$2 + 8 + 9 =$

$8 + 3 + 7 =$

$6 + 7 + 4 =$

0-7424-1791-3 *Daily Warmups*

Algebra

Look at the shapes shown below. How are all of the shapes the same? How are the shapes different?

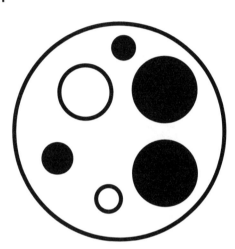

Geometry

Find each shape in the design below it.

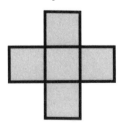

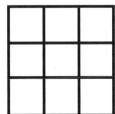 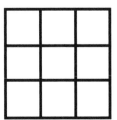

Number and Operations

Line up 10 colored candies. Write in order, from left to right, which candy is first, second, third, and so on, to the end.

Geometry

Shade the figures to keep each pattern going.

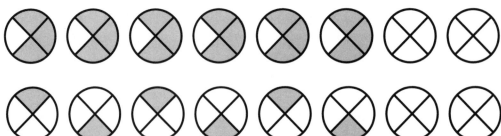

0-7424-1791-3 *Daily Warmups*

Patterns and Functions

Draw shapes to continue the pattern below.
Use letters to show the pattern.

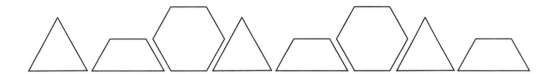

Measurement

A gram is equal in mass to one small object,
such as a paper clip. Identify about how
many grams there are in each set shown.

Patterns and Functions

Continue the number pattern.

2, 4, 6, 8, _____, _____, _____, _____, _____, _____

What is the pattern?

Number and Operations

Add or subtract.

6 + 6 =

8 − 5 =

3 + 9 =

11 − 6 =

Patterns and Functions

Draw shapes to continue the pattern. Use letters to show the pattern.

Number and Operations

Write in the numbers in the tens place and the ones place.

9 tens, I one   _____ _____ = _____

I ten, 4 ones   _____ _____ = _____

6 tens, 2 ones   _____ _____ = _____

88 = _____ tens   _____ ones

Statistics

Count the number of each shape. Then color one square on the graph for each shape.

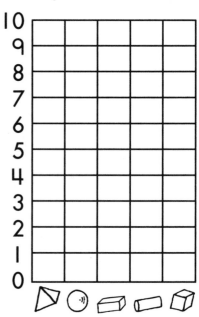

Patterns and Functions

Continue the number pattern.

3, 6, 9, ____, ____, ____, ____, ____, ____

What are you counting by?

0-7424-1791-3 *Daily Warmups*

Number and Operations

Write the correct number for each fraction.

_____ out of _____ are white.

_____ out of _____ are black.

Logical Reasoning

Which picture doesn't belong?

Why doesn't it belong?

0-7424-1791-3 *Daily Warmups*

Patterns and Functions

Continue the number pattern.

5, 10, 15, 20, _____, _____, _____, _____, _____

What are you counting by?

Number and Operations

Write the value of the coins shown below.

0-7424-1791-3 *Daily Warmups*

Number and Operations

Aisha has 2 black skirts and 7 blue skirts. How many skirts in all does Aisha have?

Algebra

Look for a pattern. Then fill in the missing numbers in the OUT row.

IN	2	4	5	6
OUT	3	5	6	

What is the rule?

0-7424-1791-3 *Daily Warmups*

Patterns and Functions

Continue the number pattern.

4, 8, 12, 16, _____, _____, _____, _____, _____

What are you counting by?

Number and Operations

Color the fractions.

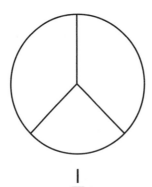

$\frac{1}{3}$ $\qquad$ $\frac{2}{4}$

0-7424-1791-3 *Daily Warmups*

Number and Operations

Add.

55 + 32 =

47 + 21 =

37 + 51 =

65 + 34 =

Measurement

Look at a 1-liter measuring cup filled with water. Then answer yes or no to the questions.

Is 1 liter of water enough to take a shower?

Is 3 liters of water enough to have a drink that will quench your thirst?

Is 15 liters of water enough to fill a swimming pool?

Algebra

Look for a pattern. Then fill in the missing numbers in the OUT row.

IN	1	3	5	7	9
OUT	2	4			

What is the rule?

Measurement

In each pair, which is the number that is an example of the lighter weight? Remember that 1,000 g = 1 kg.

400 g	40 kg
3,000 g	5 kg
20 g	20 kg
800 g	1 kg

Number and Operations

Subtract.

$15 - 10 =$

$83 - 52 =$

$69 - 45 =$

$64 - 41 =$

Measurement

Count the number of cubes.

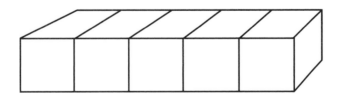

How many cubes are there?

0-7424-1791-3 *Daily Warmups*

Number and Operations

When his parents were at a yard sale, Brett saw a comic book that he wanted. He had $0.35 in his pocket. The comic book cost $0.30. How much change did Brett receive?

Number and Operations

Write the numbers in the tens place and the ones place.

46 = ___ tens ___ ones

29 = ___ tens ___ ones

71 = ___ tens ___ ones

21 = ___ tens ___ ones

13 = ___ tens ___ ones

Measurement

Count the number of cubes.

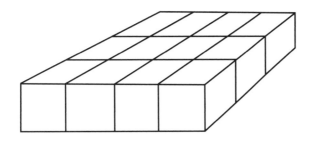

How many cubes are there?

Number and Operations

Write five numbers that are greater than 41 and less than 59.

0-7424-1791-3 *Daily Warmups*

Number and Operations

Color $\frac{1}{2}$.

 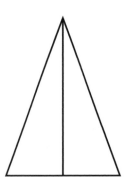 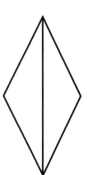 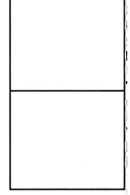

Measurement

Shaun eats lunch at noon. He is back in class 30 minutes later. What time does lunch end?

Algebra

Complete the pattern by drawing the missing shapes.

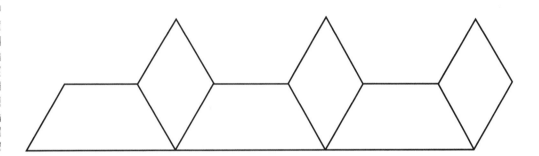

Measurement

Read the number on each thermometer.
Then write the number.

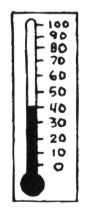

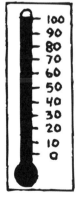

_____ degrees   _____ degrees   _____ degrees

Algebra

Fill in the missing numbers.

Number of Frogs	Number of Smiles
1	1
2	2
3	
4	
5	

Measurement

How many squares are in each shape?

inch	

_____ square inches

Number and Operations

Maya's cat had 5 black kittens and 2 white kittens. How many kittens are there in all?

Geometry

Choose two of the shapes. Compare them.

How are the figures alike? How are they different?

0-7424-1791-3 *Daily Warmups*

Statistics

Count the number of spots on the turtle.

Color the boxes to show how many spots.

1	2	3	4	5	6	7	8

Measurement

How many squares are in each shape?

cm			

_____ square centimeters

0-7424-1791-3 *Daily Warmups*

Measurement

Circle the number in each pair that is the heavier weight. Remember that 1,000 g = 1 kg.

5,000 g	6 kg
800 g	2 kg
99 g	1 kg
5 g	5 kg
6,000 g	3 kg

Geometry

Put tangram pieces together to make squares. How many different ways did you make a square?

Statistics

Look at the graph. Draw the number of shapes shown on the graph.

Shapes	1	2	3	4	5	6	7	8	9	10
Triangles	■	■	■	■						
Rectangles	■	■	■	■	■	■	■			
Squares	■	■								
Circles	■	■	■	■	■	■	■	■	■	■

Number of Shapes

Measurement

Look at each thermometer. Then write the temperature.

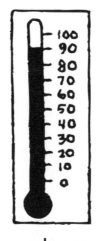

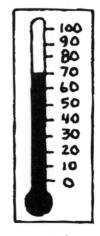

_____ degrees   _____ degrees   _____ degrees

0-7424-1791-3 *Daily Warmups*

Number and Operations

Use **<** or **>** to show which number in each pair is larger or smaller.

60   49

36   53

24   21

Geometry

Look around your classroom. Find three things that are ovals. Draw them.

Logical Reasoning

Look at the numbers in the IN and OUT rows.
Then write the rule.

IN	1	2	3	4
OUT	5	6	7	8

Algebra

Fill in the missing numbers in the OUT row.

IN	1	2	3	4
OUT	3	4		

Number and Operations

Joshua has 4 blue shirts and 2 white shirts.
How many shirts in all does Joshua have?

Measurement

Measure each brush using a
centimeter ruler.

_____ cm

_____ cm

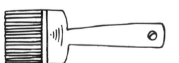

_____ cm

Measurement

How many square centimeters are in the shape below?

cm					

_____ square centimeters

Algebra

Use 10 attribute blocks.

Sort the attribute blocks into two groups. How did you sort your blocks? What is another way you could sort them?

0-7424-1791-3 *Daily Warmups*

Patterns and Functions

Continue the number pattern.

1 , 3, 5, 7, _____, _____, _____, _____, _____, _____

What is the rule?

Number and Operations

In Alyssa's neighborhood, there are 7 white frame houses and 5 red brick houses. How many houses are there in all?

Number and Operations

Add.

+

Algebra

Circle two animals in each row that are similar in size.

0-7424-1791-3 *Daily Warmups*

Measurement

Which do you think is heavier? Circle the item that you think is heavier.

a folder or a stapler

a book or scissors

a marker or a calculator

Number and Operations

Amanda has 12 quarters. Andrew has 7 quarters. How many more quarters does Amanda have than Andrew?

0-7424-1791-3 *Daily Warmups*

Number and Operations

Color $\frac{1}{4}$.

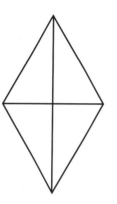  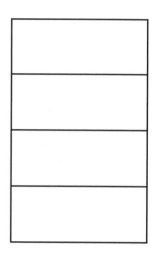

Number and Operations

Subtract.

$64 - 40 =$

$87 - 12 =$

$81 - 21 =$

$48 - 27 =$

0-7424-1791-3 *Daily Warmups*

Algebra

Fill in the missing numbers chart to solve the problem.

Number of Seals	Number of Eyes
1	2
2	4
3	6
4	
5	

Statistics

Count the spots on the turtle.
Color in the boxes to show how
many spots the turtle has.

1	2	3	4	5	6	7	8

Measurement

Look at the clocks below. Then write the time.

_____   _____

Number and Operations

Add.

$50 + 12 =$

$16 + 13 =$

$37 + 40 =$

$24 + 21 =$

Number and Operations

Write four number sentences that have an answer of 3.

Algebra

124

Circle the animals in each row that are similar in size.

0-7424-1791-3 *Daily Warmups*

Problem Solving

Use the clues to find the missing number.

 Clue 1 There are more than 5 children eating sandwiches at a picnic.

 Clue 2 There are fewer than 8 children.

 Clue 3 There are not 6 children.

Number and Operations

Write < or > to compare each pair of numbers.

135   181

110   102

104   140

Geometry

Look around your classroom to find triangles and squares. Tally each one that you find. Did you find more triangles or squares?

Number and Operations

There are 3 plates. Each plate has 5 cookies on it. How many cookies are there in all? Draw a picture to show your answer.

Geometry

Shade each shape in the design below it.

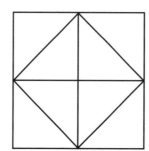
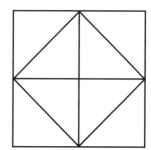

Problem Solving

Use pennies, nickels, dimes, and quarters. Show at least three ways to make $0.25.

0-7424-1791-3 *Daily Warmups*

Measurement

Irina starts her homework at 3 P.M. If she works for 30 minutes, at what time does she finish?

Logical Reasoning

Use the clues to solve the problem. An even number of mice found a chunk of Swiss cheese.

 There are more than 4 mice.

 There are fewer than 10 mice.

 There are not 8 mice.

0-7424-1791-3 Daily Warmups

Measurement

Circle the correct amount of liters to fill each container.

I L   I5 L   2 L   20 L

Geometry

Look around your classroom for cylinders. (Cylinders are shaped like a soup can.) List as many cylinders as you can find.

0-7424-1791-3 *Daily Warmups*

Number and Operations

Write the fractions.

_____ out of _____ are dotted.

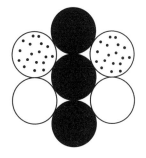

_____ out of _____ are white.

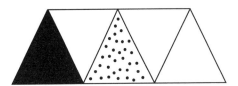

Measurement

Circle the weights that are lighter.
Remember that 1,000 g = 1 kg.

3,000 g	2 kg
8 g	3 kg
5,000 g	4 kg

0-7424-1791-3 *Daily Warmups*

Geometry

Look around your classroom to find spheres. (Spheres are shaped like a ball.) List as many spheres as you can find.

Algebra

On Puddlejumper Pond, the beavers are building dams. Fill in the missing numbers.

Number of Beavers	Number of Legs
1	4
2	8
3	
4	
5	

Measurement

Use a centimeter ruler to measure the pencils shown below.

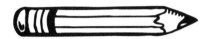

about _____ centimeters

about _____ centimeters

about _____ centimeters

Problem Solving

Imagine that you have $0.50 in your pocket. Draw two ways to make $0.50.

Geometry

Look around your classroom for rectangular prisms. (A rectangular prism is shaped like a long box.) List as many rectangular prisms as you can find.

Problem Solving

Imani found 20 apples in the fruit bowl that her mother keeps on the dining room table. More than 10 apples are red. Fewer than 7 of the apples are green. Show the apples.

Problem Solving

There are 4 coins in a cup. The value of the coins is $0.21. What coins are in the cup?

Measurement

Measure each hot dog to the nearest inch.

about _____ inches   about _____ inches

about _____ inches

Algebra

Find the pattern in the numbers. Fill in the missing numbers in the OUT row.

IN	10	8	6	4	2
OUT	9	7	5		

Write the rule.

Measurement

How many square centimeters are in the shape shown below?

____ square centimeters

0-7424-1791-3 *Daily Warmups*

Geometry

Look around your classroom for things shaped like a pyramid. These are called triangular prisms. List as many triangular prisms as you can find.

Problem Solving

There are fewer than 15 people in the hall. More students than teachers are in the hall. There are more than 2 teachers. Draw the people in the hall. Use a seperate piece of paper.

0-7424-1791-3 *Daily Warmups*

Statistics

Tally each number.

9	**12**	**17**
3	**15**	**7**

Patterns and Functions

Look at the pattern shown below. Then draw the figures to complete the pattern.

0-7424-1791-3 *Daily Warmups*

Number and Operations

Write the fractions.

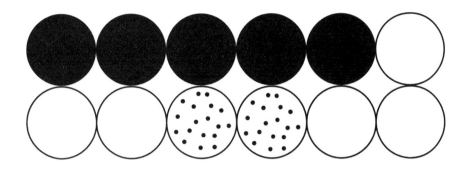

_____ out of _____ are black.

Measurement

Circle the weight that is heavier.
Remember that 1,000 g = 1 kg.

10,000 g	12 kg
40 g	4 kg
2,000 g	1 kg

Patterns and Functions

Look at the figures shown below. Then draw figures to complete the patterns.

Geometry

Look around your classroom for spheres and triangular prisms. Tally each one that you find. Did you find more spheres or more triangular prisms?

0-7424-1791-3 *Daily Warmups*

Problem Solving

In Seiji's rose garden there are fewer butterflies than bees. There are more than 6 butterflies. Draw the butterflies and bees.

Algebra

Look for a pattern in the numbers shown below. Then fill in the missing numbers in the OUT row.

IN	10	8	6	4	2
OUT	8	6			

Now write the rule.

Number and Operations

Write the value of the coins shown below.

Number and Operations

There are 4 desks in the first row of Ms. Integer's classroom. Each desk has 3 books on it. How many books are there in all? Draw a picture to show your answer.

Measurement

How many liters of water are in the birdbath?

5 + 3 =

159

Problem Solving

Lamar has fewer than 15 pencils, but he has more than 8 pencils. Some of the pencils are red. Some of the pencils are blue. Draw Lamar's pencils.

160

Measurement

Vivika's green balloon was 8 centimeters long before it was blown up. After it was blown up, it was 22 centimeters long. How much longer was the balloon when it was blown up?

Number and Operations

Write the value of the coins shown below.

0-7424-1791-3 *Daily Warmups*

Measurement

Use a ruler to measure five objects
in, on, or around your desk.
Write the name of each object where
it belongs on the chart below.

Shorter Than a Foot	About a Foot	Longer Than a Foot

Statistics

Look around the classroom to find ovals,
circles, rectangles, and triangles. Tally each
figure that you find. Then make a graph to
show your data.

Number and Operations

Color . . .
the first mouse blue.
the second mouse green.
the third mouse yellow.
the fourth mouse purple.
the fifth mouse orange.
the sixth mouse red.

Patterns and Functions

Look at the sets shown below. Cross out the pattern that does not belong with the others.

0-7424-1791-3 *Daily Warmups*

Number and Operations

Add or subtract.

$15 - 8 =$ $6 + 9 =$

$18 - 9 =$ $8 + 9 =$

Statistics

Look in and on your desk. Count how many books, pencils, pieces of paper, and erasers you have. Tally each item. Then make a graph to show your data.

Algebra

Use cubes and a balance.
Find equal values.

Put 3 red cubes and 2 green cubes on one side
of the balance.

Put 4 blue cubes and 1 purple cube on the other
side of the balance.

Write the equation.

Patterns and Functions

Use cubes.

Begin with one cube. Add cubes around it to make a
pattern. Draw and color to show your pattern.

An example:

Number and Operations

Write four different number sentences that have an answer of 5.

Measurement

Find out how far it is around each figure shown below.

_____ cm   _____ cm

2 cm

4 cm

3 cm   3 cm

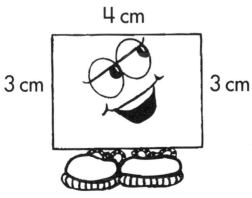

4 cm

7 cm   7 cm

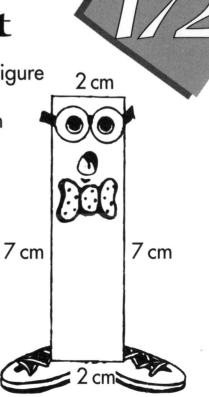

2 cm

0-7424-1791-3 *Daily Warmups*

Number and Operations

Charlayne swam 17 laps in the pool. Marisol swam 23 laps. Who swam the most laps?

Geometry

Look around your classroom. Find all the triangles and triangular prisms. Are there more triangles or triangular prisms?

Problem Solving

Erika has more than 4 pieces of licorice.
She has fewer than 10 miniature candy bars.
She has a total of 16 pieces of licorice and
candy bars. Draw Erika's candy.

Number and Operations

Anselmo stole 31 bases. Naoko stole
29 bases. Who stole fewer bases?

Measurement

Your mom is serving watermelon! How much would you rather have?

5 g   500 g

Problem Solving

Sakura has fewer than 15 fish. There are 5 green fish. The rest of the fish are blue. Draw Sakura's fish.

0-7424-1791-3 *Daily Warmups*

Number and Operations

Write the value of each set of rods and units.

_____ tens   _____ ones   _____ total

_____ tens   _____ ones   _____ total

Number and Operations

Nia picked 5 tomatoes, and Sterling picked 4 tomatoes from their family's garden. How many tomatoes did they pick in all?

Measurement

Write the time shown on each of the clocks shown below.

_____   _____

Logical Reasoning

Use the clues and color each square.

Clue 1 The second square is green.

Clue 2 The first square is not red.

Clue 3 The last square is brown.

Clue 4 The fourth square is orange.

Clue 5 Red comes before orange.

Clue 6 The fifth square is not yellow.

Clue 7 The remaining square is blue.

0-7424-1791-3 *Daily Warmups*

Problem Solving

Kara has more nickels than pennies. She has $0.26. Draw Kara's coins.

Geometry

Find the perimeter of each figure.

_____ cm   _____ cm

4 cm

3 cm   3 cm

4 cm

4 cm

7 cm   7 cm

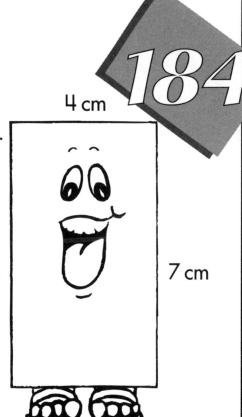

4 cm

Number and Operations

Mark bought a guppy for $0.23 and a goldfish for $0.34. He gave the cashier 3 quarters. How much change should Mark receive?

Measurement

Write the time that is shown on each of the clocks below.

_____   _____   _____

0-7424-1791-3 *Daily Warmups*

Problem Solving

Draw two ways to make $0.36.

Number and Operations

When Jacob and Samantha washed dishes on Monday, they used 25 liters of water. On Tuesday they used only 14 liters of water. How many fewer liters of water did they use on Tuesday?

0-7424-1791-3 *Daily Warmups*

Algebra

Look for a pattern. Then fill in the missing numbers in the OUT row.

IN	1	2	3	4	5
OUT	4	5	6		

Then write the rule.

Measurement

Circle the correct amount of liters to fill each object.

1 L   250 L   1 L   20 L

0-7424-1791-3 *Daily Warmups*

Problem Solving

Emil has fewer than 15 frogs. There are 5 orange frogs. The rest of the frogs are green. Draw the frogs.

Number and Operations

Martina had 16 crayons. She broke 9 of them. How many crayons did Martina have left?

Measurement

Evita and her friends played in her family's pool for 2 hours. When they played, 32 liters of water splashed out of the pool. During the rest of the week, 4 liters of water evaporated. How many more liters of water went out of the pool by splashing?

Number and Operations

Write the fractions.

_____ out of _____ is black.

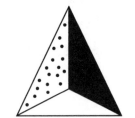

_____ out of _____ are black.

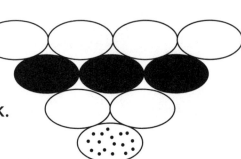

Measurement

Sofia is at the park with her friends. It is 10:00 A.M. Sofia's mother will pick her up in one half hour. What time will it be then? Write the time on the clock shown below.

Number and Operations

Dashaun and Joseph decided to see who could eat more hot dogs. Joseph ate 10 hot dogs. Dashaun ate 7 hot dogs. How many more hot dogs did Joseph eat than Dashaun?

0-7424-1791-3 *Daily Warmups*

Logical Reasoning

Ashley and three friends are in line to go down the slide.

Ashley is between Lieu and Jada.

Lieu is behind Ashley.

Marisha is behind Lieu.

In what order are the girls lined up?

Algebra

Look for a pattern. Then fill in the missing numbers in the OUT row.

IN	1	2	3	4	5
OUT	2	4	6		

0-7424-1791-3 *Daily Warmups*

Statistics

Ask 10 people in your classroom to tell you what is their favorite color. Tally the results. Then make a graph to show your data.

Number and Operations

Michelle has 19 books.
Jeff has 41 books.
Tina has 25 books.
How many books do they have in all?

0-7424-1791-3 *Daily Warmups*

Problem Solving

Use the clues to solve the problem.

Clue 1 There are fewer than 15 ants on a peony bush

Clue 2 There are more than 12 ants.

Clue 3 The ants can be put into groups of 2.

Patterns and Functions

Use cubes to make a pattern:

green, yellow, orange, green, yellow, orange

Now use three other colors to make your own pattern.

0-7424-1791-3 *Daily Warmups*

Problem Solving

Use the clues to solve the problem.

Clue 1 There are more than 5 chickadees on a tree.

Clue 2 There are fewer than 10 chickadees.

Clue 3 There is an odd number of chickadees.

Clue 4 There are not 9 chickadees.

Number and Operations

At Roberta's pet store, Jennifer bought 8 rabbits, and Julie bought 9 rabbits. Roberta started with 20 rabbits. How many rabbits does Roberta still have?

Number and Operations

Manuel saw 11 Canada geese by a pond. When one of his neighbors started to feed the geese, 7 more geese joined them. How many geese were there in all?

206

Measurement

Carly visited her friend Mariela three times this week. On her first visit, Carly brought 1 liter of orange juice. On the third visit, she brought 2 liters of juice. If Carly brought 5 liters of juice in all, how much juice did she bring on the second visit?

Number and Operations

Write the value of the coins.

Problem Solving

Use the clues to solve the problem.

 There are between 11 and 14 lizards lying in the sun.

 The lizards can be put into three equal groups.

 There is an even number of lizards.

0-7424-1791-3 *Daily Warmups*

Measurement

Add each sum. (Remember that 100 centimeters equal 1 meter.)

71 cm + 12 cm =

32 cm + 59 cm =

13 cm + 25 cm =

55 cm + 45 cm =

Number and Operations

Write the value of the coins shown below.

0-7424-1791-3 *Daily Warmups*

Algebra

Use cubes and a balance.

Put 1 purple cube and 4 red cubes on one side of the balance.

Put 2 green cubes and 3 blue cubes on the other side of the balance.

Write the equation.

Number and Operations

_____ out of _____ are white,

or _____ are white.

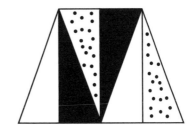

_____ out of _____ are white,

or _____ are white.

0-7424-1791-3 *Daily Warmups*

Problem Solving

On the table in Mr. Silkscreen's classroom are red crayons, blue crayons, and yellow crayons. There are more red crayons than blue crayons. There are fewer blue crayons than yellow crayons. Draw the crayons.

Number and Operations

In one month, there were 43 adult dogs at the humane society's shelter. There were 11 fewer puppies than adult dogs. How many puppies were at the humane society's shelter?

Measurement

Circle the clock that best matches what each sentence describes.

Carlos wakes up each morning at this time.

Carlos's family sits down to eat dinner at this time.

Carlos goes to bed each night at this time.

Problem Solving

Rima has between $0.20 and $0.30. Of her coins, 3 are pennies. Draw the amount that Rima has.

Number and Operations

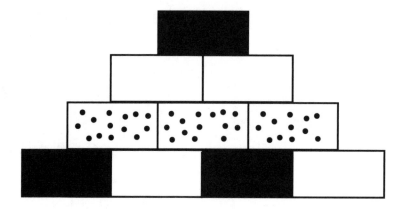

_____ out of _____ are white, or _____ are white.

Number and Operations

Show three ways to divide the sandwich in half.

Measurement

Write the time shown on the clocks below.

_____

_____

Logical Reasoning

Use the clues to solve the problem.

Clue 1 There are fewer than 20 spiders.

Clue 2 There are more than 10 spiders.

Clue 3 The spiders can be put into groups of 5.

Number and Operations

Add.   Subtract.

$3 + 7 + 4 =$ $13 - 9 =$

$6 + 4 + 6 =$ $11 - 5 =$

$8 + 6 + 4 =$ $15 - 8 =$

Problem Solving

Draw four ways to make $0.70.

0-7424-1791-3 *Daily Warmups*

Logical Reasoning

Joel has a bag of marbles. There are fewer than 16 blue and purple marbles. For every blue marble, there are 2 purple ones. There are more than 6 marbles.

Draw the marbles.

Number and Operations

What is the value of each set of rods and units?

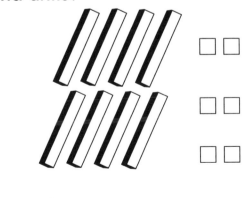

_____ tens   _____ ones   _____ total

Number and Operations

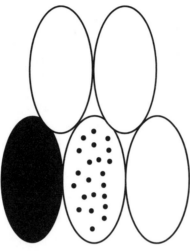

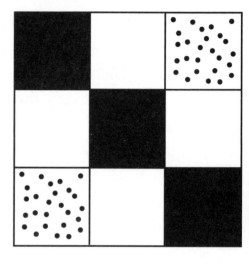

____ are white.   ____ are white.

Patterns and Functions

Look for a pattern. Use the pattern to help you fill in the missing numbers.

Number of Lily Pads	Number of Frogs
1	2
2	4
3	
4	
5	

Number and Operations

Write four number sentences that have an answer of 9.

Problem Solving

Draw four ways to make $0.67.

0-7424-1791-3 *Daily Warmups*

Number and Operations

Chelsea has 4 pencils, 2 pens, and 1 box of crayons in her desk.

Courtney has 5 pencils, 3 pens, and 2 books in her desk.

Kaitlyn has 3 pencils, 2 pens, and 1 ruler in her desk.

Who has the most things in her desk?

Who has the fewest things in her desk?

How many things do the girls have in all?

Algebra

Look for a pattern. Use the pattern to help you fill in the missing numbers.

Number of Mud Puddles	Number of Children
1	5
2	10
3	
4	
5	

0-7424-1791-3 *Daily Warmups*

Measurement

Measure each gift using a centimeter ruler.

____ cm   ____ cm   ____ cm

Algebra

Use cubes and a balance.
Find equal values.

Put 3 orange cubes and 4 red cubes on one side of the balance.

Put 6 blue cubes and 1 yellow cube on the other side of the balance.

Write the equation.

0-7424-1791-3 *Daily Warmups*

Measurement

Measure each item using an inch ruler.

_____ inches   _____ inches

_____ inches

Logical Reasoning

Hassan has 5 coins in his pocket. The value of the coins is $0.40. What are the 5 coins that Hassan has?

Answer Key

Page 6
#1: Answers will vary.
#2: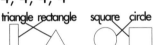

Page 7
#3: 100; 20; 10; 4
#4: 4; 2; 3; 5

Page 8
#5: Emily, 4; Brandon, 6; Latoya, 9
#6: Amalie, Mei, Matt

Page 9
#7: 7; 8; 2
#8: 6; 6; 7

Page 10
#9: 4; 4; 4; 4
#10:

Page 11
#11: 1; 0; 1; 2
#12: strawberries; bananas; 4

Page 12
#13:
#14: 2:00; 7:00; 9:00; 3:00; times can be A.M. or P.M.

Page 13
#15: 18, 20; 12, 13; 6, 8
#16: 15 − 3 − 12; 15 − 12 + 5

Page 14
#17:
#18: a quarter and a dime

Page 15
#19: Answers will vary.
#20: 10, 7

Page 16
#21: 6; 13; 9
#22: Answers may vary, but the carrot is not round; the hand is not one of a pair.

Page 17
#23: 7 children
#24: 4, 6, 46; 5, 7, 57; 3, 8, 38

Page 18
#25: 62; 91; 56; 42
#26: 15, 19

Page 19
#27: 28, 30; 24, 25; 19, 20
#28: $1\frac{1}{2}$ in.; $\frac{3}{4}$ in.; $1\frac{3}{4}$ in.

Page 20
#29: Answers may vary, but the dog does not live in water; the car is not a type of boat.
#30: 5, 7; 1, 5; 6, 5

Page 21
#31: 9; 4; 9
#32: Answers will vary.

Page 22
#33: 2 out 3 white; 1 out of 4 black
#34: 4; 9; 2

Page 23
#35: 12 bones
#36: 8, 8, 4; 8, 0, 2; 12, 12, 3

Page 24
#37: 7, 9
#38: Answers will vary.

Page 25
#39: 13
#40: The triplets in the top row are the same.

Page 26

#41: Answers will vary.

#42: 7, 5, 7; 4, 5, 5; 9, 5, 9

Page 27

#43: 4 brown bears, 6 white bears

#44: There are more sailboats (8) than kites (7); there are fewer apples (4) than frogs (7).

Page 28

#45: Patterns will vary.

#46: The center triangle is divided into thirds.

Page 29

#47: $0.25

#48: 5:00; 10:00; 4:30; 8:30; times can be A.M. or P.M.

Page 30

#49: The third question; explanations may vary.

#50: Two solutions: 41 or 43

Page 31

#51: 1 out of 8 white, 3 out of 5 black

#52: ⨉⨉ ⨉⨉

Page 32

#53: 15; 6; 14; 4

#54: m; cm; cm; m

Page 33

#55: $0.38

#56: 10 pears

Page 34

#57: about 6 cm; 5 cm; about 2 cm

#58: 19; 18; 17

Page 35

#59: Answers may vary, but possible answers are that the shapes are all circles or have no sides; they differ in color or size.

#60:

Page 36

#61: Answers will vary.

#62: ⊗⊗⊗⊗⊗⊗⊗⊗ ⊗⊗⊗⊗⊗⊗⊗⊗

Page 37

#63: ABC, ABC

#64: 7 g; 6 g

Page 38

#65: 10, 12, 14, 16, 18, 20; the pattern is + 2.

#66: 12; 3; 12; 5

Page 39

#67: AABC, AABC

#68: 9, 1, 91; 1, 4, 14; 6, 2, 62; 8, 8

Page 40

#69:

10					
9					
8					
7					
6					
5					
4					
3					
2					
1					
0					

#70: 12, 15, 18, 21, 24, 27; the pattern is + 3.

Page 41

#71: 2 out of 4 white, 2 out of 8 black

#72: Answers may vary, but two possible answers are the bike, because it has two wheels, or the car, because it is powered by an engine.

Page 42
#73: 25, 30, 35, 40, 45; the pattern is + 5.
#74: $0.75

Page 43
#75: 9 skirts
#76: 7; the rule is + 1.

Page 44
#77: 20, 24, 28, 32, 36; the pattern is + 4.
#78:

Page 45
#79: 87; 68; 88; 99
#80: no; yes; no

Page 46
#81: 6, 8, 10; the rule is + 1.
#82: 400 g; 3,000 g; 20 g; 800 g

Page 47
#83: 5; 31; 24; 23
#84: 5 cubes

Page 48
#85: $0.05
#86: 4, 6; 2, 9; 7, 1; 2, 1; 1, 3

Page 49
#87: 12 cubes
#88: Answers will vary.

Page 50
#89:
#90: 12:30 P.M.

Page 51
#91: trapezoid, diamond
#92: 40°; 80°; 100°

Page 52
#93: 3; 4; 5
#94: 4 sq in

Page 53
#95: 7 kittens
#96: Answers will vary.

Page 54
#97: 6 spots (boxes colored)
#98: 20 sq cm

Page 55
#99: 6 kg; 2 kg; 1 kg; 5 kg; 6,000 g
#100: Answers will vary, but there are eight ways.

Page 56
#101: Drawings should show 10 circles, 2 squares, 7 rectangles, and 4 triangles.
#102: 90°; 70°; 0°

Page 57
#103: >; <; >
#104: Answers will vary.

Page 58
#105: The rule is + 4.
#106: 5, 6

Page 59
#107: 6 shirts
#108: 9 cm; 5.5 cm; 3.5 cm

Page 60
#109: 18 sq cm
#110: Answers will vary.

Page 61
#111: 9, 11, 13, 15, 17, 19; the rule is + 2.
#112: 12 houses

Page 62
#113: 9 sheep
#114: frog and mouse; rhinoceros and hippopotamus; dog and cat

Page 63
#115: stapler, book, and calculator
#116: 5 more quarters

Page 64
#117:

#118: 24; 75; 60; 21

Page 65
#119: 8, 10
#120: 8 spots (boxes colored)

Page 66
#121: 2:45; 7:45; times can be A.M. or P.M.
#122: 62; 29; 77; 45

Page 67
#123: Answers will vary.
#124: horse and zebra; snail and slug; spider and ladybug

Page 68
#125: 7 children
#126: <; >; <

Page 69
#127: Answers will vary.
#128: 15 cookies

Page 70
#129:

#130: Answers will vary, but possible solutions are 1 quarter; 2 dimes and 1 nickel; 2 dimes and 5 pennies; 5 nickels; 25 pennies.

Page 71
#131: 3:30 P.M.
#132: 6 mice

Page 72
#133: 1 liter; 2 liters
#134: Answers will vary.

Page 73
#135: 2 out of 7 dotted, 3 out of 5 white
#136: 2 kg; 8 g; 4 kg

Page 74
#137: Answers will vary.
#138: 12, 16, 20

Page 75
#139: about 5.5 cm; about 3 cm; about 11.5 cm
#140: Answers will vary.

Page 76
#141: Answers will vary.
#142: Answers will vary.

Page 77
#143: 1 dime, 2 nickels, and 1 penny
#144: about 2 in.; about 3 in.; about 5 in.

Page 78
#145: 3, 1; the rule is − 1.
#146: 24 sq cm

Page 79
#147: Answers will vary.
#148: Answers will vary.

Page 80
#149:

THL IIII	THL THL II	THL THL THL II
9	12	17
III	THL THL THL	THL II
3	15	7

#150: triangle, circle, square, triangle

Page 81
#151: 5 out of 12 black
#152: 12 kg; 4 kg; 2,000 g

Page 82
#153: circle, triangle, triangle, circle
#154: Answers will vary.

Page 83

#155: Answers will vary.

#156: 4, 2, 0; the rule is − 2.

Page 84

#157: $0.85

#158: 12 books

Page 85

#159: 8 liters

#160: Answers will vary.

Page 86

#161: 14 cm

#162: $0.97

Page 87

#163: Answers will vary.

#164: Answers will vary.

Page 88

#165: blue, green, yellow, purple, orange, red

#166: The three diagonal dots do not belong.

Page 89

#167: 7; 15; 9; 17

#168: Answers will vary.

Page 90

#169: 3 + 2 = 4 + 1

#170: Answers will vary.

Page 91

#171: Answers will vary.

#172: 14 cm; 18 cm

Page 92

#173: Marisol

#174: Answers will vary.

Page 93

#175: Answers will vary.

#176: Naoko

Page 94

#177: 500 g

#178: Answers will vary.

Page 95

#179: 1 ten, 7 ones, 17; 8 tens, 2 ones, 82

#180: 9 tomatoes

Page 96

#181: 9:30; 6:00; times can be A.M. or P.M.

#182: yellow, green, red, orange, blue, brown

Page 97

#183: 5 nickels, 1 penny

#184: 14 cm; 22 cm

Page 98

#185: $0.18

#186: 4:30; 11:30; 6:30; times can be A.M. or P.M.

Page 99

#187: Answers will vary.

#188: 11 liters of water

Page 100

#189: 7, 8; the rule is + 3.

#190: 250 liters; 1 liter

Page 101

#191: Answers will vary.

#192: 7 crayons

Page 102

#193: 28 liters

#194: 1 out of 3 black; 3 out of 10 black

Page 103

#195: 10:30 A.M.

#196: 3 more hot dogs

Page 104
#197: Jada, Ashley, Lieu, Marisha
#198: 8, 10

Page 105
#199: Answers will vary.
#200: 85 books

Page 106
#201: 14 ants
#202: Answers will vary.

Page 107
#203: 7 chickadees
#204: 3 rabbits

Page 108
#205: 18 geese
#206: 2 liters of orange juice

Page 109
#207: $0.56
#208: 12 lizards

Page 110
#209: 83 cm; 91 cm; 38 cm; 100 cm (= 1 m)
#210: $0.93

Page 111
#211: $1 + 4 = 2 + 3$
#212: 2 out of 5 are white, or $\frac{2}{5}$ are white; 2 out of 6 are white, or $\frac{2}{6}$ are white.

Page 112
#213: Answers will vary, but one possible solution is 9 red crayons, 5 blue crayons, and 7 yellow crayons.
#214: 32 puppies

Page 113
#215: 7:00; 6:00; 8:00
#216: Answers will vary, but it is possible to have more than 3 pennies.

Page 114
#217: 4 out of 10 are white, or $\frac{4}{10}$ ($\frac{2}{5}$) are white.
#218: It is possible to divide the sandwich in half vertically, horizontally, or diagonally.

Page 115
#219: 3:45; 10:45; times can be A.M. or P.M.
#220: 15 spiders

Page 116
#221: 14; 16; 18; 4; 6; 7
#222: Answers will vary.

Page 117
#223: Three solutions: 3 blue, 6 purple; 4 blue, 8 purple; 5 blue, 10 purple
#224: 8 tens, 6 ones, 86

Page 118
#225: $\frac{3}{5}$ are white; $\frac{4}{9}$ are white.
#226: 6, 8, 10

Page 119
#227: Answers will vary.
#228: Answers will vary.

Page 120
#229: Courtney; Kaitlyn; 23 things
#230: 15, 20, 25

Page 121
#231: 3.5 cm; 7.5 cm; about 2.5 cm
#232: $3 + 4 = 6 + 1$

Page 122
#233: about $2\frac{3}{4}$ in.; about 2 in.; about $2\frac{1}{2}$ in.
#234: 3 dimes, 2 nickels